# THE LAND OF GOLD

# THE LAND OF GOLD

## WITH A MONASTERY OF LIGHT

Sebastian Barker

ENITHARMON PRESS

First published in 2014
by Enitharmon Press
10 Bury Place
Bloomsbury
London WC1A 2JL
www.enitharmon.co.uk

Distributed in the UK by
Central Books
99 Wallis Road
London E9 5LN

ISBN: 978-1-907587-71-9

Enitharmon Press gratefully acknowledges the financial support of
Arts Council England through Grants for the Arts.

British Library Cataloguing-in-Publication Data.
A catalogue record for this book is available
from the British Library.

Designed in Albertina by Libanus Press
and printed in England by
Antony Rowe Ltd

'Golden' betokens what is not patient of tarnish.

David Jones *The Sleeping Lord*

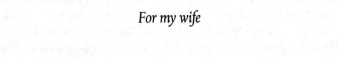

*For my wife*

# ACKNOWLEDGEMENTS

Grateful acknowledgements are made to the editors of the following publications, in which most of these poems first appeared. *Acumen, Dream Catcher, Temenos Academy Review, The Rialto, Poetry Scotland, THE SHOp* (Ireland), *The Evansville Review* (USA), *Hard Times* (Germany), *Life Lines: Poets for Oxfam* (Audio CD), *Tears in the Fence, nth position* ezine, *The Recusant* ezine, *The Dark Horse, Stand, The Bow-Wow Shop* ezine, *Sophia, This Life on Earth, The Tablet, HQ Poetry Magazine: The Haiku Quarterly, Poetic Pilgrimages: James Hogg at Eighty* (Poetry Salzburg, Austria), *The Editor: An Anthology for Patricia Oxley* (Rockingham Press). My special thanks to Michael Glover for publishing 'A Monastery of Light' in his ezine *The Bow-Wow Shop* as well as in limited edition book form.

The David Jones watercolour *Villa des Palmiers* (1928) is reproduced on the cover by generous permission of Nicholas Elkin and Sarah Williams, trustees of the Estate of David Jones. Our warm thanks to them and also to David Archer of Austin Desmond Fine Art, who kindly lent the transparency of this work.

# CONTENTS

# 1

## UNDER THE ELDERBERRY TREE

## THE HUNTING OWL

If it were possible to write
        The words I know I knew I meant,
Not lie, half ill, throughout the night,
        I would count myself content.

But as it is, true silence reigns.
        The *borealis* tints the night.
The moon invades the windowpanes
        And checks the floor with light.

No hunting owl corrects my thought
        But flies it to a spinney nest
Where skinny wings lie curled and taut
        Around the beating infant breast.

## A COCKTAIL ON COS

The waves of the sea hurry in one direction
Like a herd of cattle heading to a farm.
Couples stroll along the streets, hand in hand,
Languorous arms draped over acquiescent shoulders.
A group of children bounce a yellow ball
On grey dust. And the ever present sun
Flattens on the horizon. The hills across the sea
Roll off into the lilac haze of Turkey.
A bus, blaring a loudspeaker, advertises a nightclub.
A young boy with folded arms cycles past.
The palm trees like open fans accept the moods of the breezes
Which fail to disturb the rat-a-tat-tat of a television.
Everywhere the sound of the unkillable *bouzouki*
Redeems back gardens, bars, hotels, even as a cockerel
Protests his ancient rites. The nearby concrete mixer
Is empty and pointed at the sky.
And a gliding sparrow swoops low over a rooftop.
Come, I said, do not be shy. Take a glass of *ouzo*.
The day has been a long one. Nor may the night be predictable.

## LINES INSCRIBED ON A CORNERSTONE

Though I am stone, I once was made of thought.
From head to head I went. How then did I
Achieve resilience in the winter wind?
Who gave me hope? Who loved me in despair?

Who trusted me? Who saw me as I am?
I was a child lost in the city square.
I was a man unhinged by broken dreams.
I knew the limits charity had pegged

And walked the desert infinite beyond.
I saw my love was like a shattered skull
And passion damning what it could not heal.
But always in my heart I thought of you

Who read me now and know all solemn dreams
Dreamt for the love of others come to fruit.

# THE CRITICAL FACULTY OF THE POET

Improving what was previously better,
None too sure of what it wants to put,
Collapsing truth by pulling out a letter,
And lameing music by cutting off a foot.

Inserting meaning where none ought to be,
Feeling sure that spelling, syntax, grammar
Are more employer than employee,
Nailing the crucifix with logic's hammer.

Harping, chiding, squabbling, snarling, stabbing,
Mauling what it cannot love or praise,
Distempering the pure, while none too quietly grabbing
Whatever suits its foul and foolish ways.

The critical faculty at length cleans out its gun.
Without its fierce resistance no war of love is won.

## ODE TO MUSIC IN A TIME OF SUFFERING

Unsuffering music outside this ear
    May no disharmony of mine
Or of any other, however small or voiceless
    In the evening of the city,

Intercede in the ruling of your globe
    Encircling us all;
And may the cage of the common breast
    Robbed in a revelation of its tenderest prisoner,

Not crack or crease your countenance,
    But add to its meditation,
Which, like a cradle, holds
    An impression of Saint Cecilia.

# THE BROKEN STRING

O love I am so lonely, I am trembling in my desire
    Not to say anything. I can hardly move. My arms and legs
Are drugged and heavy. When I lie down I see you
    Cavorting in the sunny rain and laughing. What shall I do?
Everywhere I turn rings with the hollowness
    Of no love, no love at all. Why am I here? Do you know?
Have I any purpose to perform? So Sappho rubbed her eyes alight
    With pain and drank tasteless wine with friends so lucid
Daylight and the blue horizon shone through them, her love
    Forever leaving on the waves, towards the west, towards
The intolerable truth of another heart. Stay with me, stay with me
    In the spirit world, comfort me with flagons, with apples,
With all the sad absences I know too well are dreams.
    Why did you smile and look with those eyes upon me,
As though I were human and all you ever wanted to love?
    You have torn my heart into taffeta
And set it in the air of our departing,
    For always I will see you leaving
Who are too lovely to inhabit homes or hopes.
    The *aurora borealis* and the gold-capped waves
Clamour for recognition, but you are not there,
    Only the beach and the deep clear sky
And a breeze of worthless freshness.
    What will I do? My arms rebel against their labours.
I have no joy in invention.
    My life is strewn with roses from other people's happiness.
There is marriage everywhere.
    The blackbird has a nest and four young fledglings.
My garden is filled with young birds
    Pulling worms and flapping their wings.
One has even enquired to the cause of my unhappiness,
    And the worm moved in her beak as if to speak as well.

What shall I do with all this marriage of spring,
   The ducks in pairs, the uprushing fevers in the stonefaced toad?
And who knows more of union than the frog?
   Dark and terrible are these single contemplations.
*Hieros gamos, hieros gamos.* What is the cuckoo calling?
   And why is the thrush so pretty?
The sons of the wind shake hands with the daughters of the trees.
   What is the sound that restores
The joys of the infant and the brows of the wise man?
   What are the diphthongs of two silences
And the commas of the leaping antelope?
   Where are the hills whose valleys give them praise
And the house trees full of children?
   And how is the tumbleweed rolling?
I am down in the absences. Where? Where, did you say?
   Oh nowhere, nowhere. Your eyes burn through my night.
But look at me, I cannot help but love you,
   Out of tune with misery as you are.
Listen! I know I am only one person and the world shines at your feet
   But I love you. I love you till the end of all love songs
And all the lute work through the lattice windows of the churches in Brittany.
   Oh how will I break this chord without breaking my heart?
I have never loved anyone as much as you
   Yet you turn on the wind and sail away
Like a coloured kite whose broken string beckons to all.

## RECALLING LOST WEEKENDS

Wordsworth put Tintern Abbey in a poem.
Oaks claw the grassy banks of the Wye,
Wind chills the lichened arches of the ruin.
For three days I wander around, drunk,
Sober only to be drunk, yellow and violet
Blossoms welcoming corrosive drizzle.

## HOMO SAPIENS

If, to be alive, I am alive,
And if the witness to this
Is I, myself, watching the grass grow,
What is the meaning of the river?

Why does it sparkle, why does it twist
In a slow meander, why do the weeds
Grow into islands, why is the sun
Sucking it into the sky?

Long have I dreamed
On the borders of creation
But seldom have I seen
The meaning of the river.

Now it is clear,
Established by the ages,
The river is myself,
An artery of the sky.

## WATER FALLS

Water falls from the sky.
    Rivers sweep to the sea.
The world is saying goodbye
    And you are departing from me.

Rainbows loop over the world.
    Salmon leap up the stream.
All vanishing-acts, I am told,
    Are a philosophical dream.

What goes, returns, like water
    Falling from the sky
Out of the heavens, here after
    We live, we dream, and we die.

## SCORPIO RISING    TEN ZONULETS

Scorpio rising
In a great wheel
Over the house
Where I write this,

I add my love
To ice on the grass,
The Pleiades sparkling
For us.


## LOVER

softly the duvet
the piled pillows
caress your dream

even the world
grown tired with excess
looks on you kindly


## SIESTA

My love is in her chamber.
O sacral sea, crystal coast,
Seize the mind!

## A ROOFTOP IN MARSEILLES

When the sun came over the mountains,
I rose from the sheets and threw open the shutters
On the four corners of the world of your body.

## SOFT AS A DEWDROP RESTS HER SEX ON ME

Soft as a dewdrop rests her sex on me.
It is everywhere at once, and shapely.
The contours she moves in ignite geometry
To definition. But all its lines and angles,

Circles and quadrants, cannot contain the poise
She radiates. With art's long fingers, I
Draw down those curves no science may conceive,
Nor morbid poet, in his cups, believe,

Being, as they are, *extempore.*

Soft as a dewdrop rests her sex on me.
Computed by computers, she is not so shapely.

## SLOWLY THE MOON

Slowly the moon drifts over the sea.
Slowly the stars appear in the crystalline night.
Indoors, music captures the tangible happiness
In which we lived, a man and a woman in love.

Now the moon glares through tempestuous clouds.
Rain beats on the empty balcony.
How soon it was all over, the loving caresses
Fading into darkness, as the storm winds howl.


## THE BLOOM

Unsatisfied with my mind as it is,
I crave the ecstasy of wine, juggling
Sun and sea in the first sweet
Succulations of the night.


## CV

How quickly
A CV
Turns into
An obituary


## PRAYER

The unconscious
Thee Unconscious
O Thee Unconscious

## THE POET'S BODY

In a glass cathedral,
The poet's body, fleshless and boneless,
Is the nerves in outline,

The human harp
On which the hand of poetry
Plucks each word by the altar.

# AUTOBIOGRAPHY

I waded in the shallows, watching sticklebacks.
Later, at school, I learnt how to compose
Sticklebacks out of words and numbers
To set them free in the river of my mind.

Later, the oceanography of water
Came in handy, as I sailed
The world, a water-boatman on the globe
Of unfathomable reason.

The world, too true, was tricky,
But the one inside me more so.
So I drank the wine of oblivion,
A familiar face in every port.

One day, in the mirror, I saw myself,
A composition of words and numbers,
Broken blood vessels and grey hairs.
So I said to myself, it's time to be off.

And out on the long river of my mind
I sailed to you in the tremendous
Oceanography of the sea
Outside myself, you graced on the quay at dawn.

## SKELLIG MICHAEL

How bleak the observance of truth.

Sail me over
The sky to Iona,
Columba in his cell
Triumphant among the chickens.

I am going
Where Columba went
Into the rhetoric
Of the wide open sky.

Cuthbert knew it
The glory of God
In the pulsation of the sea.

The Skellig Michael
Monks got it
Perfectly. The love
Of God soaring
As the knives of the Vikings
Went in.

## SCARLET ROSE

*On the death of my grand-daughter shortly before her birth*

Scarlet Rose, Scarlet Rose,
out of the darkness, look how she glows.

Fingers and forehead, her lips and her toes,
life in its origin, look how she grows.

'I am the child of the sun and the snows
made in the making all motherhood knows.

Reach out and touch me before I disclose
the rain in the wilderness where I repose.'

Scarlet Rose, Scarlet Rose,
look how she gravitates, look how she glows.

Scarlet Rose, Scarlet Rose,
gone in a moment, gone where she goes.

# THE BALLAD OF TRUE REGRET

Never to look on the clouds again,
Never the flowers, nor seas.
Never to look on the sparkling rain,
Nor Easter in the trees.

Never to tread on the forest floor
Mottled with pools of light.
Never to open the kitchen door
To walk in the starry night.

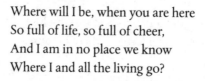

Where will I be, when you are here
So full of life, so full of cheer,
And I am in no place we know
Where I and all the living go?

What of the sound of the distant bells
Announcing a man and wife?
What of the children collecting shells
On the beach at the start of life?

What of Gloucestershire burning blue
As far as the eye can see?
What of the table set for two
With a candle burning free?

Never to look in those smiling eyes
Where my sweetheart is to be found.
Never to look on the morning skies
With the dew of the night on the ground.

What of the lakes where the wild swans glide
And the moorhens dart in the reeds?
What of the woods where the goslings hide
And the rabbits are nibbling seeds?

Never to watch how the wild wind blows,
Nor the rainbow takes to the sky.
Never to see how a daughter grows,
Nor a son, to a parent's eye.

Never the honeyed yoghurt
Spooned by the jocular don.
Never the finished work of art
With the artist looking on.

Gone are the many moments
Like snowflakes into a hand.
Gone are the blissful, intimate scents
Of love in a vanished land.

## THE GRAND DUCHESS OF PHILOSOPHY

Out of sorts with myself for over a year,
Fading fast in the slowly gathering
Decrepitude of old age, I ensconced myself
With a table and chair in a silent garden

On the sunny side of France, to drink the
Hot rays of sunshine toasting the forest.
There she was, my old friend, the Grand Duchess
Of Philosophy, snipping out my picture

Of the world with a pair of invisible scissors
To reveal the truth hidden from my mind
Long taken up in practical applications.
As on the road leading to the palace of truth

In the poem of Parmenides, I saw her
Standing in all her glory by the open door.

## THE GROUND

*for Patricia Oxley on her 70th birthday*

The poem comes and lodges
    in the editorial ear
And speaks out loud for everyone
    and everything to hear.
The roses in the attic
    are glowing in the dark.
What might have been their nemesis
    becomes their vital spark.
*So sad to be going, so sad to be gone.*
*What is the ground I am walking on?*

When looking on the great way
    that leads us to our end,
Fear only paths that lead astray
    from the uncommon friend.
We'll meet up in the Shakespeare's Head
    in Holborn, drinking wine,
As slants of dusty sunlight
    make up a chatty shrine.
*So sad to be going, so sad to be gone.*
*What is the ground I am walking on?*

My dearest Patricia
    I see you sitting there
With witty wisdom knocking down
    the icons in the air.
Drawing on a depth of mind
    both catholic and zen,
You've a quarter of a century
    showing *Acumen*.
*So sad to be going, so sad to be gone.*
*What is the ground I am walking on?*

How sweet it is to look at you
    and see you looking back
Beyond the cycles of the moon
    or the trials of the track.
Silent in a silent gaze,
    the word becomes the sound
Of a busy London public house
    where the way ahead is found.
*So sad to be going, so sad to be gone.*
*What is the ground I am walking on?*

We'll be here tomorrow
    when the rocks of time are dust,
Climbing to the terrace
    of the sunrise of the just.
Never will our memory
    or reason let us down.
We are leaving on the light ship
    from the darker side of town.
*So sad to be going, so sad to be gone.*
*What is the ground we are walking on?*

# UNDER THE ELDERBERRY TREE

*for Lindsay Clarke*

I

## THE SONGBIRD

I cannot imagine
Life without poetry
Making a birdsong.
The songbird
Disturbs everything.

Better to be dead
Than alive among cherry blossom
That does not move us.

I am not with you long.
Enjoy me
As I turn into cherry blossom.

\*

Before I go
I want to say
Why I loved life.

It was because
Without a doubt
It was possible to love.

Gone from the world, I go
A cipher, a sign
Of happiness.

\*

Never again will the honey
Drip from my lips
Like this.

My wife
Prunes the roses,
Swinging me kisses
From the tips of her shears.

*

I do not aspire
To anything anymore.
Except being invaded by
The roses in our garden.

They invade
Like the hope of heaven
In the heart of a saint
Blind drunk on God.

*

Happy again, I prize
The perfection of a pansy
Lilac in the lovelight.

Soon I shall be gone
And you will hear
No more from the roses
Nodding in the evening light.

*

I hear the songbird
Singing in the evening.
It is the intelligence of being
Calling me back to my origin.

*

Somewhere in silence
The juice of insight
Is drunk by a monk:

The breath of God
In the lyrical blackbird
Psychotranscendentally:

O my goodness!
The smell of blossom
Corrupting iniquity
Musically!

It is so appalling
Not to be drunk
While the blackbird is singing
And the stars penetrate the sunbeam
In the orchards of paradise.

## II

## IN BASHŌ'S HUT

Where will I find you
In your hut, O Bashō?
Cross-legged on the floor
At home in a corner.

I see Bashō by his hut
Poor as a church mouse
Drinking the white snow
Falling on his gate post.

I do not understand
How Bashō's hut
Holds up the stars.

Drunk again,
The Milky Way
Cascades on my page.

\*

I am alone in my garden
Under the elderberry tree.
Bashō has gone
Three hundred and fifteen years ago.
But it doesn't make any difference to me.

He is with me
Battered and broken
With a light in his eyes
That have seen wonders.

I do not need
The tears of philosophers
Who have not seen
The waterfalls of Bashō
Cascading into poetry.

Over the rock
The water flows
Filling the lake
With fishes and rowing boats
And a wine that
Once drunk
Doesn't need to be drunk again.

Let the poetry roll
A little more easily,
Let it speak
Of the water rolling over
The rock,
The glorious river
Fanning out
Into sumptuous sea.

*

Solitary and sensible,
O Bashō,
You trod the roads
Of the Japanese islands
Looking for God.

And you found him
Over and over again
In the cherry blossom,
In the morning glory,
In the mountains,
In the waterfalls,
In the stars,
In the snow on the roof of your hut.

I see God in you.
My dear fellow,
Let us enjoy
This evening with wine and laughter
Under your favourite waterfall.

# 2

# THE LAND OF GOLD

## THE FERTILE POND

Raise an eye and lift an ear,
The glory of the world is here.

The waving grass in tender shade
Complete the ground on which it's made.

Two yellow butterflies announce
Beatitude in every bounce.

The sky is boundless with the cry
A red kite calls her loved one by.

The grass is greener than the sound
Of water running through the land.

The wind is singing in the brain
Watching trees becoming sane.

Love is knocking on the mind
The blades of bracken shake to find.

The swifts around the fertile pond
Delight in that which they have found.

*nature*
*&in poetry*
*of nature*
*earth*

# THE HOUSES NESTLING IN THE HILLS

Touch the earth and feel it free
The spirit of its poetry.

Volcanic forests clothe the land
Moulded by their maker's hand.

*clouds*
*insects*
Floating clouds enrich the sky,
A silent music gliding by.

*berries*
*peaches*
The busy wasps enquire of each
Rotund and summer-tumbled peach.

*leaves*
Berries of juniper surprise
Worlds of blue delighting eyes.

*love*
*the*
*heavens*
No greener leaves employ the wind
Than those inside my watching mind.

Lords of laughter, stately vines
Rise as royal light declines.

The stars in majesty proceed
Throughout the night to spell the creed

Of what is true and lovely brings
Hand to hand in wedding rings.

The story of the force of love
Never can be told enough.

The radiance of dawn distils
The houses nestling in the hills.

## THE LAND OF GOLD

Before me lies the Land of Gold
The Praying Mantis, God, foretold.

Fields of wheat reflect a sun
Inside the mind of anyone

Who sees these forests, where the stone,
Lime white, cradles rivers down

From granite mountains, where the fire
Of earth erupted in the air

And made volcanoes grown so vast
They disappear in the mist.

Horizons blue as this are made
By those in whom all debts are paid.

Green and yellow, blue and white,
The land and sky are our delight.

Butterflies caress the flowers
Over which an eagle soars,

Its shadow on the rocky track
On which a cricket leaps, its back

Two open wings so fiery red
They barrel fire through my head,

Tick, tick, tick, the lonesome sound
Cicadas clearly understand.

On yellow dust, the brambles roam,
The berries black. The purple plum

Rockets fruit from rocky soil
Directly to the hungry soul,

Fruit so rich, the nutty trees
Bend and circulate the breeze.

Rolling rivers skinned with flowers
Meander through this land of ours.

The goats have gone. Their spoor remains.
The clouds are filled with thought. The rains

Descend. The Land of Gold is green.
The soaking trees rejoice, serene.

The heat returns. The golden wheat
Becomes the bread the people eat;

A dung beetle across the road
Pulling and pushing his earthly load.

The heat returns. A wall of cloud
Smashes, lightning thunder loud.

So saturate with heat, the sky
Turns green itself. The awful eye

One mass of dense and deadly power,
Ice cracks from its heart of fire,

And hailstones large as golf balls bounce
And bounce and bounce and bounce and bounce

On spongy lawns beside each house
Thronged by bat and man and mouse.

# THE WINDMILL

Turning on its tower of stone,
The windmill binds us to its own.

The golden fields of wheat have gone
To sacks of flour, moving on

To bread, and wine so icy cold
It rejuvenates the old

Together with the young, who sit
With bread and wine to meditate

The planet earth and dinner where
A balcony of wholesome air

Dispatches misery and grief
To settle on a floating leaf

Blown from an oak tree. In the garden
The arguments of starlight harden.

And huge, a silver saucepan, the
Big Dipper sets the trippers free.

The boundless atmosphere, the brain-
Built immensities, remain.

Vicissitudes of earth long gone,
The sacks of flour are moving on.

Turning on its tower of stone,
The windmill binds us to its own.

## CICADA

Cicada, clinging to a tree,
Sawing through my brain to be

More like a carpenter of song,
Correct my world for being wrong,

And let me sing a song for you,
The instrument of being true.

All day in labour in the heat
You sing your song you hope to meet

Sung by another, rich and rare,
As you are in the summer air,

Pronouncing precisely how to be
Vibrating in a shady tree.

Clouds float by. Their shadows pass
Like judgements on the greenest grass.

Bushes thick with insects thrive.
The rosehips nod. Your world's alive.

So thank you, sawing words of praise
For she who listens all your days.

## THE STAR OF LEARNING

Grinding and grinding in the midday heat,
The poem advances on steady feet.

Plums roll down the road. The sky
Is every inch the apple of my eye.

The sky's illusion of a veil of blue
Is nothing less than summer coming true.

Beyond, the Star of Learning speaks to me
In language geared to his machinery.

Gently the breeze cavorts with fruit and nut,
And nothing in my memory is shut.

All the doors are open. The truth walks in
A dry stone wall vacuous of sin.

Mosses dry along it. The uphill climb
To the spectacular ascent arrives on time.

*Charolais* and *salers* grace the shadeless field.
At every turn, a calvary of rusty steel.

There's music in the silence as deep as that we hear
Forming in the audit of a composer's ear.

Stone abounds. The summit can not be far
Beyond the reach of the Amazing Star,

Nowhere visible but everywhere alive,
The shaper of the spirit, before we come to love.

He is the Star dancing at my feet,
The Star of Sunlight in the shady heat.

Cockroaches and scorpions, a horse's tender eyes
Battling with assiduous and testy flies,

Conjugate the landscape, the sun-boiled hill,
The incendiary cicadas at it still.

What is at the top? The heat pours down the gold
From the furnace of the sun to his immortal mould.

## THE HANDLE OF THE SETTING SUN

Cutting through the undergrowth,
The light of reason comes to birth,

The saintly light which forests have
Before the coming of the grave.

More than sunlight settles down
Through leaves and trees to touch the ground.

It is the intelligence of light
Speaking to us through a life.

All I've been is here arranged,
The sacred forest nowhere changed.

All is as it was before
I was old or young or born.

Seated on a mossy stone,
What I was I have become.

All is solitude and prayer,
The sanctuary of a seer.

The sun lights up the moss and flashes
Through my scattered dust and ashes.

Nowhere in the azure sky
Is anything which comes to die.

The hand of reason settles on
The handle of the setting sun.

## THE CRIME AND THE CLOISTERS

Cloudy day. The sunny fields
Have gone. Two brown-backed eagles

Cry out over the forests.
Blackbirds flutter from their nests.

The stony track leads to the
Cowbell-jingling *charolais*.

The structure of an oak tree
Holds the wild wind's symmetry.

There's nothing in the high sky
But clouds enveloping my

Vision of the River Lot
Hidden in the gorges. Yet

The spirit of the river
Breathes out endlessly over

The contours of the green causse
Spiritual forgiveness.

The crime is done. Forever
There is the need to forgive.

The darkest nights that we have known
Left nothing to be thought or done,

The principle of black despair,
The slaughtered bodies everywhere.

The fall of man was not a
Storybook nor the slaughter.

Faith is to believe in face
Of everything that is the case.

The ancient stones glow with moss.
High on a ridge of the causse

I track the voice of the word
Heard in the song of a bird,

Speaking to me through the stones
A huge caterpillar climbs,

Laughing in the butterfly,
Walking in the fields nearby,

At ease with me under these
Summer cloisters of oak trees.

## THE CRUCIFIX

Deep in the gorges of the Lot,
I walk the runway of the heart.

The palaces of power obtain
Their power from the river's rain.

The power of rain itself becomes
Oranges, lemons, geraniums,

The garden-brightened cut-stone homes,
The mountainside the hiker roams

Looking down to see the river,
Green as olive oil, forgive her.

In the woods, the trees are still
Solar panels of chlorophyll.

Down in the valley, the light is green
Breathing the sky. The grass is clean

As a mind swept of everything
But the waving grass in the wind.

Green is the walkway in the wood.
Green are the groves where a building stood.

Green are the palaces of mind
Once city-rich, now nowhere to be found.

Alone on a rock in a quiet glade
A golden stone crucifix displays

The power of nature to be true,
For golden is the lichen hue.

Above, a fire of blue ignites
The sky. It is heaven in its rights.

## TREADING TILES OF SUNLIGHT

Today, tomorrow, yesterday, the heat
Pours down redemption on my sandalled feet.

Dandling on the stony track, the shade
Pronounces the hieroglyphs of praise,

So subtle the butterflies repeat them,
And the oak trees in the sun reveal them.

Out of the forest, they appear
Two young and lightly nibbling deer.

Their fiery orange pelts vibrate,
Their hind legs bent for the escape.

Towards me, in the bramble-prickly field,
They walk – delicately – nose deep in leaves,

Unafraid to look at me, and I delighting
In creatures so innocent and pure, they bring

Praise to perfection, as their luscious eyes
See the same around them, as their lips prise

Dark green leaves from a bush, before they move on
Back to the forest from the shining sun.

Praise is the corporate of man, when he
Escapes from himself. The cicadas agree.

Dressed to kill, the forest abounds with light,
The *viriditas* of God everywhere in sight.

Mushrooming like armies, the oak trees shield
The crumbling walls of the long-abandoned field.

Everywhere – oasis. The gift of song
In stone and moss alike, as I walk along.

Praise is the engine of the rolling soul
On pilgrimage to heavenly thought in control.

Down the aisle, between the trees, I go
Treading tiles of sunlight on the grassy road.

## THE MISCREANTS OF PRIDE

Summer in the landscape breathes with ease
The supernatural articles of peace.

We long for what we most desire, the war
Of open-minded lunacy no more.

Stars encircle paradise on earth.
At dawn, the oak trees witness it on oath.

Soon the dew is lifting, as the haze
Promises the pledges of the rose.

The great judge sun, robed in silky cloud,
Listens to the miscreants of pride.

Lies as large as continents deny
Denial is the culture of the tribe.

The jury is the passageway of time
Identifying every single crime.

The verdict is the values of the man
Hanging on the cross in the judging sun.

# THE BROKEN STONE

'Atone, atone,' the broken stone
      cries out, but no one hears.
'I was once as you are now,
      the envy of my peers.

'The vineyards here were absolute,
      the wine as rich as rain.
Stones were carved and houses built.
      The luxury was plain.

'For years and years, man tilled these fields
      and reaped the juicy crops.
Hand to mouth, the wines were drunk
      and sold from global shops.

'It was a plenitude so kind
      churches rose of rock
Shaped like an angel's house with God
      in every granite block.

'And then a wind which blew from far
      beyond our wildest dream
Crushed our paradise on earth
      I beg you to redeem.

'Within the wind a germ was found,
      a fungus made of mind-
Destroying elements, which took
      the kindness from the kind.

'Famine lashed the land. It drove
        men to emigrate, half mad,
Looking on the ruined fields
        of what they thought they had.

'Atone, atone,' the broken stone
        cries. 'The famine comes
In wind of such a magnitude
        it crops these broken stones.'

## THE BURIAL OF PRIDE

As I walk in the shade of the afternoon,
      the crickets leap aside,
Part of my unearthly procession
      to the burial of pride.

The oak trees join me standing still. The flies
      add a whirring music.
The *Mantis religiosa* supplies
      the camouflage mystique.

The sun redoubles its effort to ignite
      the white rock. And fire
Breaks from the stones, a visionary light
      the proud ones desire

To work their wills on the populations,
      exploding it
In the soft underbelly of the nations
      for formal profit.

Geared to God, a prophet is a man
      the crickets leap aside,
Part of his unearthly procession
      to the burial of pride.

# THE QUERCY CROSS

There in the shade of the Quercy causse, the cross
Stands, as the bells of St Jean de Laur float over
The green auditorium of thin oak trees.
Patterns of sunlight rearrange their colour

As the wind strokes the oaks and settles down
To the fructification of the forest.
The sun pierces the leaves and stings the ground
With baking pools of stone in this neverest

Of ecclesiastical ascension
Towards the stone cross smacked with gold fungus,
An aureole of butterflies, the neon
Blue of the jet-threaded sky, the cicadas

Penetrating literature, with sharp teeth
Biting out the substance of my living breath.

How changed it is since the rains came down,
The rains so many and so various
They drenched the land, catherine-wheels of water
Cascading down the hills and through the trees,
Bowling through the villages, till even
The lizards were flushed from their hideaways
And shook on flat stones, inspecting the
Solemn wonder of rain. Now on the track
Rich brown earth leaves trails of fertility;
And the moss cries out on the dry stone walls
Ecstasies of sunlight. The thin oak trees
Dazzle, the mellow green of the grass
Amplified by the gentle light. Tree tops
House a cacophony of crows. There is
A stillness in the forest anchored to
The mossy roof of a shepherd's stone hut.
Cicadas ply their trade. The Quercy causse
Is not magic. It is the high road to
Compostella or the high road from it.
       Here in the French landscape is beatitude.
The causse drops away to the river valleys
Under a blue horizon. The geologist
Notes millions of years in the land's formation.
Now, in the long dry grass, the cicadas
Erupt in the blazing sun. The grassy track
Unveils the veneration of a pilgrim
Winding through the woods. Trees give sustenance
To the air and the mind of the pilgrim.
There is a three hundred and sixty degree
Gateway to the opulence of God, flashed
In the dart of a lizard, in a world
Gone mad with murder and mad opinion.
       Slowly the path brings us to the cloisters

Where the assembled oaks entrance the entrance
Of a wiser way. Here is serenity
We imitate in the stone cathedral.
There is more than man could devise in the
Sheer brilliance created by the sky,
The trees, and the grass. The music of the wind
Surpasses understanding, the rich glow
Of the quenched moss the very bed of green.
The oak trees juggle particles of light.
There is a hymn humming in the cloisters.
The soft ceiling of the trees shades the grass.
Branches of oak are quilted with bright green moss
And a trellis-work of silver lichen
Laces the berries of the juniper.
               Ravishing as water to the thirsty,
The cloisters are a haven in nature
For the poetry of contemplation.
Recognition is the mind of a monk
Kneeling on stone, an ecclesiastic
Kneeling beside him, for from these cloisters
Rose the stones of the dizzying cathedrals.
For these are the Quercy cloisters, guarded
By a host of crosses and calvaries.
               It is a sacred nature, our inheritance
From the fathers and mothers of the church.
A yellow dragonfly loops around a tree.
Grass glows on the long greenery of the track.
A night of torrential rain has sent
The red deer running over the stone walls,
Thudding hooves disappearing in the bush.
Alone with this superabundance, I
Relish the red radiance of a berry
In the mud. The causse grows dense with seeds

Proliferating everywhere, a hive
Of birdsong. Here is a clearing for oak trees,
A truffle grove, with a manless stone hut
Looking out over piles of sawn timber
Gathered long ago. There is an air
Of detachment between man and nature,
Nature closing in as the oak trees sprout.
　　　　　Beneath the track, the limestone drops away
In a grand geology of hollows
Through which the water runs. The caves are as
Cool as larders, jewelled with dripping stone.
In the Pech Merle cave, the painted horses
Scintillate through time. The spirit rises
From the dead, our intrepid ancestors,
Twenty-five millennia in the dark,
Now a bright painterly light in the caves.
The causse is breathing. The ground drops away
Down a gorge deep as fifty million years
Have moulded, now a long-abandoned mine
For the lustrous phosphates. A black beetle
Searches round my sandal, the rain-filled earth
Without another footprint. The sun lights
An oak tree, a mossy candelabrum
Brightening the sky. Nowhere's as serene
As treading on the causeway to the cross
Transcendentally still in the lunchtime heat.
　　　　　Washed by the rain, the lichen on it glows
Like the gold beginning of life on earth
When the rocks had formed from the sun-tossed ball
Of incandescent magma. Out of the breath
Of God, the minerals of making formed
The cellular constructions of the leaves
I see around me. On the Quercy cross

The lichen of the golden age remains.
The cross forgives. The lichen on it knows
The cross was there before the world was made
And radiates the thought. In the virgin earth
The print of a mountain motorbike betrays
The thinking of another kind of life.
The silence broods. The blue planetarium
Responds with sunlight in the airy trees.

# THE WALKING HEART

The road to the miraculous meanders
Through the living forest to the water
Fallen from the sky and the high mountains.
The fat river slides under the low bridges,
Swollen with the miracle of rain.
Silver fishes sparkle in the sun
Seen by an elder's eye on the long walk home.
Brighter than the greenery of paint,
The rain-intoxicated trees and moss
And grass and grove and glade and field, sing
Out of the love on fire in the walking heart.

## THE GARDEN OF THE POEM

Here is the garden of the poem,
The place where love and language meet.
What was the language of us and them
Has become the contemplative seat.

As the sun lifts the shadows from the oaks,
The grass is mottled with so bright a light
The orchard of mossy trees evokes
The presence of a panic-banished sight.

Tremendous accolades of leaf announce
The burning furnace settles down to this,
The murderous sun becomes the speckled place
Where sanctity and sanity are bliss.

Trembling in the breeze, my soul on fire
Wanders in the garden in the summer air.

## THE WALKWAY

So green and faraway the groves
    so present to me now,
So rich with green fertility
    in every sunny bough.

Water, wild and wonderful,
    has been and washed the stones
Along the mossy walkway
    I trod my dying bones.

Love as magnified as this,
    green in the green green trees,
Knows no fear or appetite
    to worship or appease.

The love of God is raining down
    in sunny summer air,
And I am on my own to write
    the ecstasy I share.

Love was on the walkway
    in every step I took
Walking in the forest
    with my pen and my book.

I wrote for you what I admire
    in the spirit of the mind.
Nothing is so beautiful
    as sight to the blind.

In every step I took I saw
    the spirit of my Christ
In every nook and cranny,
    in every oak tree, blest.

## THE LAND OF GOLD RETURNS

The Land of Gold returns. I see
    it flashing in my brain,
The yellow leaves on dainty trees
    before my eyes again.

This is the land which God foretold
    the just and the good.
It is the land called paradise,
    the soul, the sacred wood.

I enter with my eyes lit up
    by a paradise so fair
I am alive to every scent
    in the embracing air.

I thank my God that I was born
    to walk in paradise.
It is a country of the mind
    no poet ever lost.

For poetry is what it is,
    this paradise on earth,
The Land of Gold, in which our lives
    become what they are worth.

# 3

## THE TABLETS OF THE BREAD

# THE TABLETS OF THE BREAD

### 1

Our lives seem so immense to us, our littling and eradication by death are more to us than the puncturing of inflated balloons. They are the hurt and the anguish of the unappreciated. For death makes us feel this way. Because death has no respect for us, we are fools in all our thoughts, and mistakes in all our actions. Nothing makes us look so unnecessary as death. Nothing undoes us so efficiently, nor unweaves our webs so effectively. Death laughs at what lives, for there can be no reason for life while it is around, other than extinction. We believe, therefore, in God; and those like Ezekiel, Plato's Socrates, and Christ; because not to do so, makes us believers in death. I do not believe in death, because although it destroys, and brings the genealogies of life to dust, and the orogenies of the Peloponnese to galactic ribbons, it cannot create a simple buttercup or the Rose of Savage Landor. Death can do nothing but die.

### 2

We see it in the empty shell on the beach, or the wasp on its back
      beneath the bathroom window.
We see it in hospitals, crematoria, the graves of Abney Park.
Eagles transport it in their beaks, and the rolling wave surfs it to
      the sand and the palm trees.
Wheat is happily reaped by it, even as fighter jets spit it from the sky.
The coiled fossil in the stone recalls it, the bronze colossus
      succumbs to it, and the fragile icicle melts in its hot hand.
A rose in a buttonhole defies it, but the one on the coffin confirms
      it is the case.
Noah sailed over an ocean of it; so did British captains on the
      lucrative Atlantic, the fearsome Middle Passage.

Birds rustle in the bushes, a fluttering of life, but the forest fire engulfs
    them as it dies in the night.
There is a cry in the garden, where a tortoise munches the stalk of a
    beetroot.
Cities under the ground heard the cry, but they are dead themselves.
The cry was death in the jaws of a cat, the mouse-like noise tolled in
    the human bells.


3


Tectonic plates tremble if it touches their edges.
Big-hearted businessmen lie under its harmless paw, now invested
    in heaven.
It is, as rocks flake off the mountains of Ethiopia, and the snows of
    Antarctica slide into the sea.
Death is the tractor ploughing the killing fields of cousins.
Loud is the sound when it knocks on the gate of a now medieval castle.
Alexander the Great was great because of it, or not so.
Once it was the skulls on the doors of every hero.
We see it on battlefields, the generals turning to go.
It dies a little when the sun comes up, but, within an hour, its
    harvest is secure.
Twenty sailors chant a shanty on the songbook of the sea, chased
    by beady seagulls to the waterbed of their graves.
Somewhere in town a lock has clicked shut on the boomerang of a
    plan: twenty more are dead in the gangbangs of the brothers.
Ah, death so close it nudges at my teacup.


4


A leaning monk looks over a porphyry font, and there is a body floating.
Propped on beds of amaranth and moly, the Lotos Eaters sing the song
    of melancholy.

Clouds die in the blueness. The curious vine climbs the yellow
   trellis to watch.
I saw the rainbow coming into being over the mountaintops, as the
   anger of the sky curled up under it, dead.
The butcher is a woman seated, outside her shop of meat, by the
   smell of wood smoke burning in a field where three
   sheep graze.
There was no hope in the trombone. Its case was shut. There was
   no one left alive who knew it still existed.
Out of an olive tree gone to seed, there fell the carcass of a grasshopper,
   shining like the wings of a singing cicada.
Death boomed in the thunder of undiscovered galaxies, a thing unheard
   in Europe at the time of the World Cup.
Ticking in the beams of a church, the beetles do God's work, for God
   invited death to be the jury in his courtroom.


5


And hear the pitiless chainsaws, in the graveyard of the village, sawing
   up the olive and the cypress wood all day.
Down the rivers of the pregnant continents, fertile fish give birth to
   their meaning.
For in the belly of the dying woman the living child is born.
Death creeps over hairstyles. It is found in the lacery of underwear.
   They say that even new shoes reflect it at weddings and
   funerals.
Nor is death to be trumpeted in the ears of an irritated orchid.
Yet it may be soundly whispered to the chirpy gait of a robin.
For out of the redbreast comes a language cleaner than the Reaper,
   for out of the robin there comes the song of the birth of life.
Anthills are temples to the durability of industry, cathedrals to the god
   who sculpts the statue of death.
There is no meat in the larder, because the house fell down last spring.
We laboured over an equation: the truth was equal to itself: difficult to
   make sense of the dead mathematician.

## 6

Giraffes were galloping over the African plain, when a mongoose
out for a drink saw a python eating a pig.
Long gone were the days when the shooting parties lingered. The tents
had housed their bones in the catacombs of hollowed
limestone.
Limestone, too, was dead, the graveyard of crustacea, as numerous as
the stars in the skies of Cappadocia.
And why in the skies of Cappadocia? For there the holy fathers, in the
care of the holy mothers, glimpsed the astronomy of the
never-ending story.
For there their lustrous intellects caught fire – from the brush-torches
applied by the living death-fiends –
To shoot like dizzying rockets beyond the constellations of the ecliptic.
Star signs drowned in rivers of pitchy oblivion, although children were
born as usual to bagpipes in dancing Scotland.

7

An old man wore sunglasses because death was dazzling, but an old
woman swept by on roller skates, hand-in-hand with
wisdom, to show what wisdom is.
Thought was gathered in hermeneutic jam jars, sealed at the top with
rubber washers: death was outlawed.
Idiosyncratic language danced on dead-tight tightropes, turning into
a poetry the dead scholars were reading.
And dead to their brains as they might be, the scholars are living proof
poetry is the language of the philosophical gem, the
*margarita pretiosa.*
O scholars come to life before language is invented, an appropriate
reminder of our peopling of silence!

Too soon the time of the silicon of the handaxe.
Too soon the time of the silicon of the computer.
Too soon time as such, a friend in the evening orchard.
Too soon time as such, a midge flicked from the shoulder of an
          amanuensis of God.
Trains hurtling over bridges, into the rocks of the rivers, know the
          feeling of vertigo confirms the wings of illusion.
Strutting on Hampstead stages, prize-winning horses are neighing.
          What they admire is death in a cage on the stage they strut.
Throw out a welcome to whisky, and the vodka, on the table: they
          know the death of life in a glass is resurrection in the
          bloodstream.
And that blood which was given up for sinners, kicks the fool to
          wisdom, now quite dead to folly.
As the ship approaches, a giantess to a crib, the island harbour buzzes
          with the news.
For on the decks are angels, messengers it seems, each one holding
          wine jars and the tablets of the bread.

# 4

## A MONASTERY OF LIGHT

# THE SITOCHORI POEMS

*A Village in the Mountains of the*
*south-west Peloponnese*

Dedicated to
Vassilis & Eleni Zambaras

*Poems by Odysseus Elytis translated by Kimon Friar*

"... and in a Monastery of Light keep secure that wonderful moment when the wind scraped off a bit of cloud above the farthermost tree on land."
'The Other Noah'

"... the cerulean line of the horizon in a hue intense ..."
'The Autopsy'

"My mother was still living ..." 'The Light Tree'

AUTHOR'S NOTE

In 1983, inspired by the modern Greek poets, I drove to Greece and bought a ruin in the mountains of the south west Peloponnese for £780. The original building dated from 1789 but it had been a ruin for 60 years. With the help of the villagers, led by Agathon 'Rathana' Liatsos, I re-built the house. They and I saw to it that the restoration was done according to the old traditions. I became intimately familiar with every stone, beam, tile, pipe, wire, and so on, making up the fabric of the finished building. The inside lining of the new roof, for example, was made of bamboo. There was a garden of 500 square metres, much of it cactus. This was to be my home from home for the next 30 years.

# SITOCHORI

## 1

Lightly, as the shadows of clouds move over the mountains, I stroke
    your hair and cherish you forever.
We grow accustomed to death, as the spring flowers steal upon our
    eyes once more.
But death is a stealth bomber under the roof of our radar.
Life is a radiant highway rippling through flowers, a patina of gold –
    over an earthquake territory.
All glory then to algebra; it calculates death like the neon sign of a zero.
Death stumbled on a lilac iris, apologising for its grossness. The flower
    forgave it and turned into heaven.
The fig tree was rooted in the foundations of the house. Funny how it
    flourished on its pedestal of stone. The leaves were as green as
    Ireland, the figs as plump as plums. For underneath the rock,
    death lay sleeping.
What are the colours of the garden of the sun? Purple, white, and yellow,
    daisies in heather, gods waving to gods, with death on a leash.
Nothing has the advantage of spring in the mountains, a Grecian spring
    that is, where the gods are roadside flowers.
The gods are lamps of God, lighting the day to paradise around us.
    Death is the instructor teaching us to dance down the spiral of
    the poppy, the field of red heavens by the church where God is
    worshipped.

## 2

So manners are observed by the nightingales of Greece, wonders are
    done here, and wonders never cease.
Death is an acrobat performing in the skies. He doesn't need a net. He's
    dead already, yet, he somersaults on stilts before our very eyes.

The sun is a day-torch blotting out the stars. What is it looking for in
      this world of ours?
Death is the answer. When the sun sets, taking death with it, the stars
      appear to contemplate deathlessness.
Death is the answer. I look in the garden where my sweetheart used to
      play, now a pigsty with the droppings of a donkey on my way.
Death is the answer. The roof has new tiles. The balcony is new. The
      workmen on their ladders are hammering it to you: the former
      occupants are dead and you will be so too.
Death is the answer. Death is in the tears falling down my face when
      my daughter appears.
Standing in the morning, she asks, looking all around, Daddy, will this
      house last forever?


3


Tears are the pathos of death.
Tears, for all that exists will fail to do so.
Tears, because the time we shared together was so sweet, and now it
      is over.
Tears, because tears are the appropriate response.
Tears, because anything else is offensive.
Tears, because the glory of life is singing in the village, and the birds
      respond in kind, and the sunlight is caught in the blossom of
      the pear tree, and the valley below blooms yellow in the
      sunset, and the bees ride the honeysuckle-scented air, and
      the goat bells chime.
Tears, because without them, such beauty is invisible. For tears are the
      lens-brighteners of the eyes. Through tears we see the true
      and everlasting beauty of transient life. For to create life, it is
      surely nothing extra to make it transient or eternal.

# 4

The sink was blocked with a question even more tiring than money.
>Where does the detritus go in the larynx of the drainpipe?
>Will death make it a skylark?

Previous conceptions of death had died, and new ones took their places.

Shades of the pomegranate tree fell across the garden. The erupting vine
>was bathing in the sky. Flowers serviced insects and insects
>flowers. And from nowhere came the stone seats of the
>philosophers, all gone.

There was a great flock of white sheep on the green mountainside, their
>bells ringing in the olive grove. A butterfly landed on the stone
>table and winked its wings. Death was driving up the
>mountainside in a brand-new hearse, its engraved windows
>twinkling in the sun.

No one walked on the green lane. The cypress trees were tilting at the
>sky. Bees collected the nectar of the gods. In the valley of the
>shadow of death I wandered, with a staff made of bamboo.

I smelt the coffee in the kitchen reconfiguring my days. There was
>boundless joy in the moment. Nor did I fear to die. Heaven was
>in that kitchen and I went inside to drink some.


The glamour of the stars was in the star-shaped flowers, the Stars of
>Bethlehem. Nor did the glorious anemone disappoint, the lily
>of the valley, the mountain windflower.

Only the magpie, bright black and bright white, priest of the joyless,
>rasped the discord of the morning.

Geese were fattening. There were cockerels and hens in many a
>homestead yard. Swallows flew through the house several times.
>There was a kitten on its back. And somehow the cornerstones
>were pillars of the sky. Life was the gift of God, death did not
>come into it.

The old men round the table playing cards at night, had hair as white
as whitewash, and all their eyes were riveted to the science of
the game. Marvellous heads, as conscious as consistent, the
bright balls of laughter rolling in their eyes. Death was an old
story they all knew off by heart.

What mirror flashed an opal of light on the stone wall? It was the
glass of my watch. Somewhere intelligence was signalling to
me. There are no signs from heaven that a blind man cannot
see.
An axe chopped the living flesh of a tree. Down she came, forever,
where the builders shovelled sand, cement, and lime. And the
wind in the olive trees chanted her away, exactly herself,
forever, out of time.

There is a flat-topped mountain in the Messinian plain, where flowers
obliterate the dying in the brain. It is called Mount Ithome,
the stepping-stone to God.
For God is in the dark blue sky, the strange halo round the rim of the
village at noon, looking like radiation, turning almost black,
quietly cooking the village in a daily way.
The walnut tree is laughing in a spectacle of bliss. The builders'
hammers chip the stone walls. The fig tree gives praise. By a
table on the mountainside the valley cups the sun. Death is
the vision of losing this, made for everyone.
A fig leaf, waving through the window in the kitchen, signals the gates
of paradise are open, then shut. Locked out of Eden, sin and
death now roam, searching out the mind of man as their
official home.

# 6

When the old die, the young forget them. Yet the daisies of childhood
have not grown old. Here before me now they ride the
heliotrope of time. And when it comes to rest, young and old
are one. Death cannot undo them, nor the thunderous sublime.
I sit on a stone in paradise. The wind tosses the heads of a multitude of
flowers. The urgent birdsong tells of the time when death
stalked this valley and all the men were killed. Now the jets of
Nato drill the sky, ferocious claps announce them, the
guardians of paradise.

The sun silvers the leaves of the olive trees, filling the clouds with a
white light, and the mountain paths with upright grasses. The
smell of the washing on the washing-line is just that: paradisial.
It is what foreign travellers take home with them. There is no
sound but the cockerels crowing and the tyres of the builders'
truck crunching gravel.
The bodies mouldering in the graveyard all have names. Many were my
friends. But their true identities are alive in paradise, where God
escorts each one with the care and dignity of an usher.
God is great. It is nothing to him to do this. The identity of every star is
not a problem. Nor the fashioning of particles so small, they can
pass through the earth without noticing it is there: *mu mesons* is
what I call them.

# 7

I saw the bread on the table toasted to a charm. Beside it tuna fish and
green pepper. Butterflies collided with flashes of yellow. The air
was tangy with expectation. Any moment the village might
become the messenger of God, the angelic presence already a
tentative fact.

On the blue washing lines danced particles of sunlight. The steadfast
     moreas, pollarded and sturdy, which once fed the silk worms
     of the Silk Route, now feed the chorus of the trees, while a
     donkey thuds a hoof and a goat neighs softly.
Scoops of wind flutter the many boughs, their beauteous apparel. A
     cat treads daintily through a bed of clover. Wheat grows in the
     garden, tall and green, neighbour to the spiky artichokes.
     There is a wall of light on a crumbling house, and a porcupine
     of cypresses crowns the mountain above the church. Death is
     seen in a dead aravafna, once so pink and white, its blossoms
     like roses.
The ten thousand Stars of Bethlehem open at my feet, close in the
     evening, like the cupped hands of prayer.
The sun embosses the mountains, a choreography of contours, of
     green and yellow, and white villages, like Aëtos and Chalkias,
     Artiki and Malthi, Rizochori and Polithéa. As the last sun slips
     off the mountains, and the dark comes down, the stars and
     the villages twinkle on their own.


## 8


Death is truly rated in the conscience of the just. It is the spur to the
     horses of instruction. God will not be adumbrated by the
     minimind of man. God is in the wine jars and the tablets of the
     bread. God is in the seahorses and the resurrection of the dead.
We do not even know how we are able to digest our food. Socrates
     laughed at scientific explanations of anything under the sun.
     And quite rightly, too, because he didn't even know why the
     sun was there.
The gods of Sitochori are Christian and kind. They are not chronological,
     like Chronos. They do not swallow their children. They are the
     flowers of the roadside and the untrod village path.

Rhythm is what makes poetry in the language of the true. And rhythm is forever when the pulse of life is new.

Death is a counter-movement, a cat on the prowl, where life is brought to zero in the beak of an owl, gazing at catastrophe with a dismissive scowl, as a builder remonstrates with his chisel and his trowel.

O give me a glass of the wine called Taÿgetos. For on those snow-capped mountains no poet is at a loss. The wine is like water watering the brain, when death comes up to threaten in the Messinian plain.

In my sixty-third year of walking home to God, I met young Byron roaming the isles of Greece, looking for something to die for, Arkathía, the freedom of the Greeks.

Can there be a substance more substantial than the sound of eighty Greeks or Welshmen harrowing their ground? The ground, of course, is suffering. Eternity, it seems, is the choir of the lover, who won't give up until the suffering is over.

Give me the picture of my father on the wall, and my mother with her glass of wine, when we were walking tall. O, but not the mortal dross!

O give me a glass of the wine of Taÿgetos!

9

The asphodels are out in force, the poppies have arrived. Stone is back in fashion for the houses and the walls. The sunlight's on the mountains like a veil on a bride.

Sparrows flicker in the olive groves, hyacinths irradiating absorption into glory.

The sea stretches away like light blue silk. And the palm trees wave at
the faint discus of the moon. A long-leggèd hornet hangs before
the delicate beauty of a red valerian. The waves lap the
geometry of the pebbles. The sharp igneous rocks are stroked
by the therapy of the sea.
In earthquake territory: 'the cerulean line of the horizon in a hue intense.'
A flock of white gulls flies low over the water. The engine of the sea is
idling. Roses rushed by Interflora are not so red as these, here
at my elbow as I look around. And in a tiny chapel on the
seafront, where the restaurants are found, the candles burn all
day. An avenue of palm trees escorts me to my lunch.
The pink of koutsoupiá, *Cercis siliquastrum* (the so-called Judas tree),
outdoes Chantilly lace, erotic, spectacular, outrageous, a
miracle in pink.

A goat kid walks across the village square and kneels down beside a
blue Mercedes.

Damosels and dragonflies drink the gorgeous gorge, where green and
yellow water is translucent to the rocks, boulders of white
limestone like the spine of an ox.

10

There's a chapel in the mountains drowning in flowers.
The trunk of an olive tree is like the mind of a monk, a contortion of
rigidity and strength, holding up the olive branch and the olive
of God.
The golden-eyed goats by the blue beehives chew the rich grasses in
their long brown shaggy coats.
The news is everywhere. It's paradise today. Crowds of orange poppies
confirm it on our way.
Easter is the celebrant ringing the village bell, hanging in the plane
tree above the churchyard wall.

Out come the villagers in a canticle of black. They're coming from the
    graveyard, they're going to the church. Beyond the iconostasis,
    the priest is making prayer. The chanting has begun in
    all-embracing Greek.

O for the smell of wood smoke when it comes from the olive tree! Ten
    hens and a cockerel all flick their heads. Up climbs the vine in
    the dressing of new life. Crows caw in the cypresses. And the
    bright yellowy green of triffid-like *Smyrnium perfoliatum* amazes.
    Among the scented pines, the cones are dropping.
The garden is hedged by frangosykiá, *Opuntia ficus-indica*, a spiny cactus.
    I'm told Christopher Columbus brought it back with him.
    Because of its fecundity, like the impressive yucca *Agave americana*,
    it could also be called, but isn't, the deathless one, athánatos,
    everlasting.


11


There's nothing to match Christ's blood like the red of the red anemone,
    deeper, richer, purer than the illustrious poppy, where dialects of
    daisies dedicate the ground. The ground is a tapestry of blue and
    yellow, pink and purple, white and green, so intricate no needle
    stitched it, nor felicitous hand.
The flowers are the gods of the hillside. The birds are its choristers. The
    bees in the purple vetch, the white and yellow saxifrage, the
    violet-blue gentians, occupy my eye. The garden door is open.
    Spring walks in.
And here among the filigree of the flowers, she shows me the original
    patterns, the natural ones, of all erotic lace-work.
I take her by the hand and we walk into the house. From the scrubbed pine
    tabletop, we drink the wine of Taÿgetos, and break the bread from
    the ovens of Kopanaki.

So great is death, it seems silly to be alive,
Unless,
Unless the spell of death has been broken by the Redeemer.


12


At the touch of a finger, the loo flushes perfectly. The shower is the best
in the world, raining down freedom. The bed is totally out of
order, an orgy of the sweetness of sleep. And on the balcony,
at breakfast, the music of Mozart brings on the complexity
of happiness.

Mother of God! The asphodels adore you!

And in the village of Avlona, it is written on the road, *kalo taxidi*: have
a good journey. The fields are strewn with stones known to
the Mycenaeans, and the sun at noon is perpendicular, as it
was to them.

Of the makers and the singers I name: Nikos Kazantzakis, Mikis
Theodorakis, the genii of the Rembetika, George Seferis,
Nikos Kavadhias, Maria Farandori, Yannis Ritsos, my
favoured one Odysseus Elytis, and the nightingale of Greece
herself, Maria Callas. I notice the cats come round in the
evening, about 6:30, to be charmed by them.


13


There is an olive grove in town, by a bakery selling whisky. Children
play basketball in the school foreground. Next to it is a
football pitch of green astroturf. Hanging like lit globes in a
tree, oranges light up the street, assisted by a hedge of
pink-red roses.

There is no clock on the wall. The icons are made of sea shells. The
fridge gives off a startling whiteness. Flying in and out of the
house, the swifts are tumultuous. Crushed ice in orange
juice soothes the topical messages waving from the vine
leaves in the blue azure.

Children manage the alphabet with a prophetic surety, indicating the
next generation of car and house insurers.

Boats float by on the sea somewhere near Kyparissía.

The beach of Kaló Neró is a crescent of golden sand, empty of people,
taking in Sergiáni, where the Arkathíkos meets the sea, and
the protected turtles breed.

There is not a soul here. The sea is a transparent light green, just like
the Arkathíkos coming down from the mountains, through
its estuary of tufted reeds.

The Arkathíkos ripples like a poem where it runs over the white stones.
The flat sea is a capacious novel lipping its sentences in tiny
waves.

Sand between the toes admits of the nature of childhood, when the
eye of the mind dilated on the gorgeous grains.

What of the corncrakes crexing? And the luminous pebbles on the
lapping beach? Press me into silence, as I walk the sand, the
silence of infinity in the promised land.

What are these rocks? Where are they going? On the shoulders of God,
they sail through time to build the foundations of heaven
started on this beach. There is no toil here nor trade of any
kind. The tender waves caress the sand.

The Arkathíkos flows into the sea. The salty sea drinks the pure river
water with an oceanic thirst. On comes the river with the
opulence of God.

The songs of the swifts batter the ear through the headphones of the
sky. Stereophonic sunlight sings to the blinded eye.

# 14

Sidirókastro is set in a cup of mountains, a village crescent around an
    olive grove of buttercups and sheep. And there is the graveyard
    bedecked with crosses. And just above it a field of beehives.
    Wisteria falls over walls.

I come to the church to pray for the martyrs of Greece, for whose
    blood Christ gave his blood. Both give me the ground I
    walk on.

I can hear a bee in the vetch. It is the siesta. Green and gold smyrniums
    sway in a shadowed orchard. A crow flaps the expanding sky.
    This is a land where the donkey carries Christ every day.

Here are the mountains and the valleys to make a shepherd cry out in
    delight. For here the sheep and the goats with equal dignity
    graze, where the calls of the birds sanctify the sky. Magnificent
    the brown coat of the goat beside the white iris.

This is a place to die for under an oak tree in the spring. For here God
    has extended his hand to help us on our way – *kalo taxidi* – the
    vast orogenies, the millions of buttercups, gently persuading
    us to see things more through his eyes.

# ON THE WAY TO KYPARISSÍA BEACH AND BACK

## 1

Look at that rain puddle. You'd better be quick. It's hitching a lift on
the wind.
You see that signpost to the necropolis? Aye, the bodies once there
have hitched one too.

There's a lone crow in the milk palace of the clouds. Cypress trees sway
gently in the breeze. An old gate swings by an abandoned field.
The corridor through the mountains is hazy with mist.

You can rely on the bougainvillaea to hit your heart where it hurts. What
could be more painful than never seeing it again? It is the loved
one in planet form.
Leaves race about in the sunny air. The claws of cockerels tread daintily
over the stony yards. Music is just out of reach, as a fly interprets
the world.

## 2

There's a lizard on the road ahead warming its back in the sun. Six blue
beehives integrate with the finest orders of mechanics, the proof
of which is honey.
Vertigo enters the mind of the man who sees the abyss of God. So much
space to fall into with no gift of flying. And because there is no
bottom, the fixture is permanent. Goodbye forever, is what it
adds up to.
The mountains are arrested in an expensive coat of green. There are
more fir trees per square kilometre than there are local eyes to
count them. And there is a solitary olive tree playing to the
gallery.

## 3

Many are the nights when I lay here, on the sandy beach not far from
    the discothèque, listening to the stars and the soul of Mozart.
    There was a profusion of shooting stars almost every night.
    The watery wine at my side was the inspiration of my children,
    dancing the night away in the purple glow of the dance floor.
Now children on bicycles ride past the unspecial place.
The white walls of the waves play the instrument of the beach with
    such a musical care for the courtesy of our lives, I am thinking
    of drinking it in.
How many steps to heaven? Three, I think. I forget them all, on top of
    the starlit stair. There is no gloom to accompany me. The race
    to outer space has come and gone. I am a man awake on the
    beach, with Bach in all his glory more alive than dead.


## 4

The seashore roars with the hidden depth of scale, like the depth of
    things felt in the tremor of an earthquake.
The smell of seaweed entrances a girl on her knees.
I smell the fragrance of a rose uniquely unfolding in being. That's some
    sort of bribe, I think, and one well worth the taking.


## 5

The girls laze about looking like a million dollars. And every one is
    fairer to me than the ink-blue line of the sea in the sketches of
    an artist, under a large straw hat, drawing his inspiration from
    the Greek horizon.

Inhaling a cigarette, one sends me a smile. A light from the gaze of
   creation filters through the trees. I hear the talking, the words
   of young women, as the waves keep thrashing the beach.
   Surely they are right, these words, for they are engendered in
   the fertility of the sea.
It is not appropriate to endure the sunlight tip-toeing the terrace in the
   form of evanescent leaf prints. The code is: love it, for this is the
   time of your life.
How sweet is the custom of the barefoot walk on the beach, so
   nonchalant by the branches of palm trees, shaped to make shady
   shelters, as the white sail of a yacht perfectly investigates the
   cerulean hue.
For the time comes, when going for a walk is a thing of the past.


6


Heaven is all about us. Only the people build another world, one they
   can see and understand. Then they buy up the artist's vision,
   to say how sorry I am I did not recognise it before.
Heaven is all about us. The sun-scripted dialogues between old
   adversaries put a spice in the ice-cold beers, chip a thought to
   a sharpened pencil, stamp a yes on the magical days.
And the nights. Do not forget the nights. Do you remember the one . . . ?
   Do you remember . . . ? Ah yes, heaven is all about us.
The fish swim into the net. The seed corn multiplies. The grape crushes
   itself in its haste to become a glass of wine. Sparrows confirm it
   all, with a hop and a skip and a flight.
Heaven is all about us. The hands of the clock slow to a sleepy stupor.
   Oranges fall from the trees. Leaves bat the sun, while drinking
   it up. Cicadas are the typists in the trees writing it all down
   correctly.

Heaven is all about us. The ice-cream van has arrived and the beach is
full of children. Mothers are young once more. And the young
prince, walking on sand for the first time, publishes the triumph
of infancy over the cruellest hand. No hand dips like a mother's
to scoop up her young Buddha.

7

Everywhere the relics of the mind of man are found. Take this quad
bike, for instance. What do you make of that? And how about
that plastic bag caught in the thistlegrass?
And what of all those stones lying under the earth, which used to be
Mediterranean cities?
Is it too much to ask how we escaped all this, and came to our present
senses? Did we sail on the back of the coelacanth through the
seamless seas of sex?
As the waves pound the igneous rock, the long-established discourse
between water and fire continues. And air and earth are in
this too, as you can see. I am not making this up. I am writing
it down.

8

The Greek flag is out in Kakkaba in the Messinian plain, while all
around are the mighty orogenies turning a luminous yellow,
as the shadows of the clouds move slowly over them.
The road ekes out a course up the mountain. The breeze polishes the
olive trees. A horse flicks his ears. The cypress trees taste the
silent juice of the light. A hint of birdsong ushers in the
evening.

White cloud erupts over the mountains. A flock of sheep ambulates
in an olive grove. Vertiginous drops fall away from the
roadside. The long grasses sway. The setting sun lights up the
face of a fig tree. There are tortoises moving about.


## 9


Ringfenced goats natter as the car glides past. A lone dog barks outside
a well-worn kennel. There is majesty over Platánia to fill up the
hungry eye. The passion under question here is encyclopaedic.
What the mind cannot see, the eye cannot tell.
Here is a sight to knock you out of your noodle. For here above the
gorges of the Neda, and below the vast orogenies and the
erupting clouds, is a Greek village like home on earth. For this
is the village Platánia.
A tint of autumn is in the air. That touch of valediction. Over the sea
comes the sky. The sun is falling into his hammock. The stars
wave through the diminishing blue. The cooks are prodding
their kitchens.


## 10


And so into the village of Sitochori an entrance has to be made. Taki's
café is the target. There sits Rathana with Leonidas, Giorgio
and Taki himself. Thanos has come from Florida, and his
brother Dimitri, 71, is just off the jet from there.
Oh, what a kerfuffle there is, as Dimitri displays his skill with politics,
just a tiny bit bombastic. Taki winks, and the evening takes on
the beer and the chiparo, while the stars congregate in
amazement to oversee such human intercourse.

The full moon rises over the eastern mountains. The many cats embarrass my door. There is nothing to do but feed them, as my hand turns to the playing of music, under the ecliptic heavens.

# MARATHÓPOLI

### 1

Days. What are days? Are they links of time? Do we make them up?
There is no doubt a light wind is wrinkling the water, as caiques float
        on it in the Kyparissía marina.
But is it today or tomorrow?
And what does it mean to say it is yesterday?
The sleep of dreams divides them, and who will say that is reliable?

### 2

The sun bounces off a windscreen. A chicken wanders through an
        olive grove. A swift swoops under a telephone wire.
There's nothing on the road, before or behind.
Is this day a beatitude?
Does the Sleeping Lord wake up and walk among the olive groves?
Is there room enough here for the living God?
Who will dispel the songs of the sparrows?
The sight of light basking in the branches of a palm tree?

### 3

The bamboo drinks from the hidden river.
The road is a hairpin bend anticipating the river.
There is a trickle of more sparrows in the luxuriant foliage.
*Tempus fugit*, uncurtaining the mountains.

What is the clematis doing, blowing blue, sun-irradiated trumpets
on the edge of Filiatrá?
Shall we untangle the trunk of the olive tree to see what jewels are
hidden in it?
Do I mean money?
Who will dispose of the sea transubstantiated into sapphire?


4


The carpets of the olive groves are sun-inwoven grass.
The palm trees of Marathópoli accept the sky with the open arms of
a friend.
There is nothing tó the restaurant by the sea, except all you ever hoped
for, served with a winning smile by the tall owner.
The pace of life accelerates to a standstill.
The worthlessness of ambition sings the hymn of the sea; so as the
waves splash over the rocks, all its dreams are fulfilled. It has
turned into achievement.

Look at the island of Proti. The sun does. And the sparkling eyes of
the bay.
Could the planet be more mysterious, if Proti got up and danced?
There's octopus for lunch, drunk down with the liquid grape.


5


The places where we went together are warm with memory.
Is there a serenity more serene than the recovery of love?
Love is not the noise from a conversation. It is the conversation,
walking hand-in-hand by the sea.
The fir trees bright with Mediterranean light confirm it, as a great
freighter crosses the horizon from north to south.

Proti does indeed dance, on the evidence to the contrary.
It is a singing rhythm in the particles of the place.
It's the pet of Marathópoli, now sun-bathing on its belly in the garden
of the sea.


6


Hang on to your laptops, as the light skids into town.
Was ever a place so illuminated, with never a finger lifted?
Pour on the shore, O welcome wavelengths, there is more to redeem
than the continents heaving in death.
Give birth to the spirit of life! Of rapture!
For this is Marathópoli.

The blue horizon is sharp enough to shave with.
The great freighter is the carborundum sharpening it.

Reach out your palm and look at the light floating in it.
Twenty-five Euros per gram?
The mallet of the sun bonks you on your brainbox.
Men swim across seas, dying to get to it, paying whatever price the
journey may cost.
For once that light is in your palms, you can splash your face with it,
and the back of your neck.
There is nobody to stop this, this side of sanity.


7


Carved Byzantine rock is strewn about the place, some of it in the
church.
You can hear a file putting an edge on steel.
A man with a shovel shifts a pile of sand.
The neon light on the pharmacy blinks all day and night.

## 8

It's time for a look at the mulberry tree, the blueblack ink of the sea
      its willing audience.
'I am building a house,' it speaks, 'of solid golden stone.'
The house has a tower with a turret to one side;
And a mason with a hammer, in the middle of a huge pile of rocks,
      thinking it through.
A bus flies past, shaking the air.
'What is the point of your story?' inquires the blueblack ink.
'It's this, quite simply,' says the tree. 'The mind of man fashions the
      chaos of shapeless rocks to that magnificent golden mansion
      you can see over there. The mason is man the artist, the maker
      of beautiful form out of the common detritus.'


## 9

Come with me down the bamboo road to hit the brilliance of the sea.
Diamonds are jewels which sparkle.
But this sea sparkling under the sun makes diamonds look tame.
What the sun does to the sea, and the sea to the sun, is another order
      of being.
This is the wealth that money cannot buy.
From tycoon to beachcomber is a small step.
But what to do about death isn't, is the picture.

The sun shines on my T-shirt and I am ablaze with a kind of warm
      infusion.
For I am anyone who is listening to this.
This is the fabric of the world, before the unkempt mind of man tears
      it to pieces.

## 10

There's a single yellow parasol on the golden curve of the sand, with
    a woman lying under it, inheriting her paradise.
The sound of the sea is a madrigal in her ear.
The light breeze blows the low herded clouds into her dispensation:
    she sees what she has come for, and she likes it.

## 11

Hang onto your T-shirt, Archie, this blue sea will kill you.
There is an intensity to it – which is what it is doing in you.
This is the blue that makes sacred.
It burns you up inside and makes you a nobler spirit, the old one dead.

## 12

Here is a chapel by the sea, painted white and light blue.
Out on its little promontory of rock, the sea washes its feet.
There's not a person anywhere. The sun warms my page.
The chapel folds me in devotional spirit.
I am its animator and it is mine.

## 13

I wake up and see a bit of blue heaven in a white arch.
They are right above me. It is the truth.
I am awake in my house, and this is my morning window speaking
    to me.

1

There sits Mount Ithome on a sightline to the mouth of the Nile.
The apparatus of a leathery sky saddles the noon. The sun mounts the
      saddle and the hot light draws out further the juice of the
      grape.
There's a long scar on the mountain where the vehicles of thought
      travel up and down. Mine's a Daihatsu. Rathana's old Toyota
      has grace about it yet.
There's a suggestion of understatement in the wind in the olive trees.
A classic autumn day in the Messinian mountains rises to the climax
      of serenity in the light mist on the Taÿgetos.


2

A massive fly lands on my page and looks at my writing. I see his brain
      take it all in, before the eventual take-off.
What a glorious glide by a grey-backed crow, who voices herself to
      another as she lands on the ground.
There is a grain to the fallen walnuts, cracking open at my feet: it is the
      unseen opulence of the spirit of the tree.
The *arbor philosophica* rises in the oak raising itself to the sky rooted
      in the rock.


3

The stone walls of heaven are cemented by nuns, with the help of
      falling raindrops out of a sunny sky.
The houses in heaven aren't painted with the azure light of the dawn.
      There is no need, for the stones are of that quality.

The cars are jets. The banks cathedrals. Money is blades of grass. And
food philosophy.
The angels have all converted from left- to right-hand drive.
And God is a chef cooking up lunch in the fruit of a cactus. There's
oodles of such fruit about, on this God-given mountain track.
For this is the deathless plant, *Opuntia ficus-indica*. Its prickly red fruit,
oval to a nicety, swamps the mountainside.


4


Dimensions of beauty spring out of the seasoned rock.
There's music in the hills and iron ore.
Who can see the gold trickle of a well?
For the creator of the gold trickle of the well is the carpenter of the
bolster of being – this plain before me, where the Spartans
cropped their slaves.


5


The asphodels are like the silk mantles of the tilley lamp. The breath
of God blows in them and their response is a constant
inner glow.
There are old rocks and young ones in the family graves of the dust.
There's a tight-knitted body of oak trees where water comes down
to the track,
And many quills of bamboo.
How green is the lip-reading cypress, the chaperone of the land.

Rock melts into mud.

## 6

In the forest of the bamboo, it's like a learnèd tent, as the long stalks
     curve over the track from either side: the shade here listens to
     microscopic raindrops teaching the art of silence.
Now the full rain comes, in answer to the thirst of the erudite.
Can you hear the birds sorting out the debts of anxiety?


## 7

Here is the stoniest olive grove confronting a village farmer. It looks
     like rocks have been raining, some of them rather large.

I'll take a rest here, as the vibration of the mountain is going to my head.

The cars wind up and down the mountain stitching families together.

O lilac cyclamen under the thorny bush, speak to us all on the mountain
     of our being!


## 8

No orchard was ever so planned, nor tucked away so neatly.
It's on the end of the track near the summit of the mountain.
The chances of meeting a raptor are pretty good.

And rapacious is the appetite of the gnawing jaws of time.
One by one each of the trees is plucked of its fruit.
The timeless hands of better men than me feed the jaws with an
     affection often seen in the young.
Who are the timeless men? And are they visible?

## 9

Each one is the original from whom the visible was formed, the
　　time-wearied character, who ate and drank and died.
God, being ingenious, felt it was better this way, for upon death the
　　resurrection of each man was made so much easier.

## 10

So this is how the orchard is cleaned of its gorgeous fruit.
You can lie on the sunny grass.
You can drink the falling rain.
There is only one stipulation you must not ignore.
Thinking is not permitted except between the hours.
So you must save all yours for those happy moments when time,
　　like infant writing, is not joined up.
Drift on a cloud away. Dreaming is essential.

# IN THE FOLDED STRATA

### 1

The rain washes away the folded strata.
Where did the rain come from to manage this?
How did a ball of fire acquire such stupendous oceans?
And what are oceans? They are more than fish tanks.
Who will put a price on the meaning of the sea?

### 2

The road runs circles round the mighty Neda gorge, getting swallowed
    in the process.
The boundary lines between human, natural and divine melt in the
    meeting of mind and mountain.
There is a kind of terror in the air, the euphemism of which is panic.
What on earth are we doing on earth?
Before a single answer suggests itself, be careful you are not
    brain-washing yourself.

### 3

Nothing is obvious to the well-trained mind.
Who could transpose the contours of these mountains into the sketch
    of an ordnance survey map?
You need a genuine feebleness of imagination to walk through
    Kephalórisi, not to mention Platánia, without getting vertigo.
They say the native Americans, who built the skyscrapers, quite got
    over vertigo, and walked on them as securely as this column
    of ants on the mountainside.

## 4

But what if you're out on a limb of the body of Christ?
What if mind has mountains and mountains have mind?
How can I prevent Christ walking off the mountain with me on his arm?

Hold my hand and lead me. Lead me to my rest.

Like an anvil trembling under the constant thwock of a hammer, my
        deepest senses are shaking because of an awesome presence.
I am not far from home. I wouldn't dare be.
There is too much at stake to risk another inch.

Down from the sky flies the thought of an eagle.
The look in his eyes makes it clear what he thinks.
Is it so very different with Christ, the raptor of the conscience?

And look how his lady nests their babies!
This is Christ, too, I know.
For now the sweetness of his presence renders the mountainous drop to
        the comfort of home life.


## 5

The folded strata are the ironed sheets of God.
Time and the patience of a housewife have done a good job.
You can see the layers of time husbanded into geological order.

There is a bankruptcy in our understanding which stares us in the face.
As the mountains keep on moving, so I feel it in my bones.
What shall we do but melt into what we are?
And how unhappy it is to be gone forever.

## 6

The sky is too large for me to sit on the holy hill.
It would lift my brains off in a jiffy, like an eagle lifting a fish.
So strapped down by hoops of steel, what can I see in the distance?
Are those merry-go-rounds, by the camel trains on the Silk Route?
Are there children in rabbit fur chasing ducks to a river?
What can that possibly be, but my mother and my father joking over
       wine in the evening by an open fire?
And who's that playing a piano under the cherry blossom?
Do I see through Greece – through a crucible of holy water?


## 7

The villagers do not think I am mad. Or a smuggler. Or a spy. Although
       they used to. For it is said the British dropped gold and guns
       here in the second world atrocity.
Why did I come here? To write a poem I said. To myself. For who else
       would have believed me? Until the thing was done?


## 8

O Dimitri in the café under the roof of the rain! Where is your Florida
       now? Your grand new house with its swimming pool? Or your
       huge house here overlooking mine?
Everything has vanished, except the chiparo in your waterbottle.
There is nothing to do in the mountains, when your mind is truly
       empty, like a mystic condemned to contemplate dross, out of
       which the light of God has gone.
There is nothing to do, but argue with your childhood roots in the rock.
America gave you money – and a hole in the head for your troubles.

How wretched success! And that day in the Reno brothel!
You gambled away your life and sit in the café alone.
But I congratulated you. Because you have a spirit as generous as
    a friend.
Tough as an old goat, and never grumpy, you walk home barefoot in
    the rain.


9


So appoint me a computer to calculate the facts of the matter.
How many lives in the union between the living and the dead?
In the folded strata?

What terror, what adventure, what *meta ta physica*, pass through me
    into the day-filled night.

# PSÁRI

## 1

How tightly packed are the graves; and well walled in from the world.
The horses graze in the fields, the shadows of their tails flicking
Brushing the grass, in the Messinia Horse Park.
Who would suppose this was Greece? It looks like Virginia.
Various herds mind their own business.
Most of the noses are touching the grass.
Birds chirrup from tree to tree.

The acorns in the oak trees are falling to the ground.
There's a large flock of sheep below unworried by this.
A few bells gongle.
You can hear crows in the distance, the corporate managers of
      the plain.
The baaing of the sheep echoes in the eucalyptus trees.

A silver taxi slips past and out of sight.

And now the flock has gotten up and come to have a look at me.
Hello, my fellow mortal! they speak as one.
I reciprocate with a wave, and provoke a baa in response.
Away they go, in the hands of the good shepherd.

## 2

The crucifix on a shrine advances towards me, followed by the
      mountains turning into the believing in a solemn procession.
      *Kyrie eleison.*
For the mountains are the congregation that has gone before us – and
      returned to give us strength in our present company.
      *Kyrie eleison.*

Order returns with the olive tree taxing the earth for its oil.

3

I can see the Mycenaeans looking out from the high mountain village
    of Chalkias.
There's a mist gliding between us.
What are the upper reaches of understanding in their stony tholos
    tombs?
The shepherd's hut to my right is a stony room.
The tufted top of a bamboo stalk paints the sky.
There's a grey cloud heading south.
The heart of the world has been removed and replaced by a new one.
This is the heart of the healthy whole of heaven, ticking in the body
    of Christ, swallowed on Sundays by the Christian crew –
    sailing between earth and the holy land in that grey cloud
    heading south. *Christe eleison. Christe eleison.*

4

The kingdom of heaven is within us, as confirmed by this heart with
    a cross in it carved in the bark of a eucalyptus.
There's a butterfly in a vineyard reading the newspaper of the sky.
Drops of rain tinkle on the tin roof of my car.
There's a black dog wandering about, who has finished with despair.
How did the host of Psári account for that?
And where is the church where the fact was authorized?
– The fact that we do not die in the body of Christ.
We die outside it.
So into the body of Christ drive this Daihatsu.

## 5

Here in the streets of Psári the office of God is open for business.
A woman talks to a man. The rest is silence.
A cat walks past calor gas bottles. The square is damp.
Green umbrellas sanction an empty restaurant.

I recognise the war memorial, presided over by the goddess of
      memory, writing down the names of all those killed in battle,
      to well before Homer.
It's a work of art in marble, a frieze of modern, middle, and ancient
      Greek warriors.
An oil lamp burns on a carved pillar, to light up the understanding of
      the goddess, who is surely beautifully drawn.
There's a mountain range behind making up the backdrop of the truth.


## 6

'When did a basket hang in a tree quite so majestically?' an orange
      geranium asks, as the sun returns and a butterfly crosses the
      street to let the bus go by.
The wet patios feel no feet, for it's the siesta.

A column of cornerstones resembles a zip.
A trailer full of firewood looks good to me. For the *jaki* is the fireplace
      where the tales are told, to the children who become the
      parents, who become the Greeks.
A pollarded morea nods in agreement.

### 7

The mountains range like the rhythms of molten rock.
I'm in a tiny boat below the massive waves of a sea of stone good
    enough to let me float for a moment.
Christ puts out his hand and the mountains feed from it like lambs.
*Kyrie eleison. Christe eleison.*


### 8

Time climbs into his hammock.
A thousand years pass.
Keeping vigil over the village of Psári, its guardian angels have not
    budged an inch.
The love and praise of God is inlocked into the system.
Archangels stroll the streets at night, and especially during the day.
Psári protects its magpies, who hop from hope to hope.

# THE SEA SEEN FROM SITOCHORI

### 1

I am by the church where my son, Daniel, was baptised; and where I
      go to Mass.
Rathana, his godfather, is the regular cantor, sometimes chanting for
      three hours at a stretch.
There are new frescoes on the walls and an iconostasis respected by all.
Athos, the husband of Demitrula, was laid out here, where we all
      kissed him goodbye.
He was a barber and my neighbour, who delighted in giving me wine.
An old brass bell hangs in a plane tree, to summon the faithful to God.

### 2

What was that? A lilac anemone, a purple bougainvillaea.
The path climbs through the village.
The sun is delightful.
It is the first of October.

### 3

My house is known to the Listed Buildings Service in Athens.
I can see it from here below me.
Above me is Rathana's house, with a garden full of cats.
I'm on my way to see the sea from the mountaintop, stopping in the
      cool shadows.
There is no shortage of splendour, shining out of prehistory.
The mountains are covered in scrub oak, but their massivity irradiates
      naked power.

## 4

Thalassa! Thalassa! The beach of Kyparissía!
Only a shallow mind would not gasp.
Here is my destination, my beginning, and my end.
Kaló Neró. Sergyáni.
A milky blue horizon.
The jets of Nato vigilant for snoopers.
There's Africa over there and Italy to your right.

## 5

Sitochori is the toast of Greece.
See it in my uplifted glass tonight.
'To Sitochori.' 'To Sitochori.'
The breeze in the scrub oaks murmurs a like opinion.

The sky blue sky is washed with delicate skeins of white taffety.
To sit on a stone and observe is to be grateful for life.
The sea seen from Sitochori is grounded in love.
Chapels abound.
For love is grounded in God.

## 6

No hasty metaphysics brought me here.
It was the study of a scholar gypsy, as my father dubbed me,
         waiting for the spark from heaven to fall.
Well, here it is.
The sea seen from Sitochori is grounded in love.
The spark from heaven lights up the welkin.
The dead live on in our memories and these in the body of Christ.

The Messinian plain flows to the silky sea.
For *Christos anesti*, Christ is risen, and the evidence is here before me.
Crowds of binoculars won't see it.
It does not register on the photographic plate, chemical or digital.
It is a presence.
Take the presence of your husband or your wife or a friend – of your
        loved ones.
Each is unique and obviously so.
This is all of them put together, and many more, multiplying
        endlessly into
The presence of Christ, sensed by the intelligence of Christian faith.


7


Walking on water, the light of the sea caresses each burning forehead.
No responsibility is lost on it, warming the broken backs of the
        mountainous heroes.
Not a particle of being escapes notice in this landscape, where the
        holy terrors sniff out every pigsty.
There's one right here beside me. It's like trapped lightning in a jamjar.


8


Everywhere – acorns. The oak tree spills a seed to nourish the planet
        wisely.
There is grace in a carpenter turning it into a wheelbarrow.
Picture-framed by paradise, the Sitochorion eye sets the prospect
        in perspective.
It is the mountains running down to the sea, nursed by the many
        freeholds, with the unique of the Greek bussed in from
        the stars.
Look from here tonight and you will see what I mean.

## 9

Somewhere in London a mind dreams of this reality.
I witness it now.
I cannot take my eyes off it, as the singularity of history and the
          present meet.
I have friends in the picture, good and living ones.
They move about in the intricate patterns of their freedom.

## 10

My mother was still living, when I first came up here alone.
She was in bed in the house, with a tray of flowers on her lap.
She knew all their Latin names, although they were new to her.
My last shot of her was a picnic we had in the stadium in Olympia.
She'll be around somewhere, in a prospect rich as this.

## 11

As you turn away, villages cradled in the mountains greet your
          gaze, always understating their case.
It seems a miracle they are there.
And so it is.
For man to be born and to live, in such a place as this, is indeed
          miraculous.
This becomes more obvious the closer you are to death.